B & O THUNDER IN THE ALLEGHENIES

by Deane Mellander

Carstens
PUBLICATIONS, INC.

P. O. Box 700
Newton, New Jersey 07860

ISBN 911868-45-3

 Edited by Frederick A. Kramer and Theodore F. Gleichmann, Jr.

INTRODUCTION

I SUPPOSE IF YOU scratch a railfan deep enough, you'll find the Baltimore & Ohio to be one of his favorite roads. That's the way it is with the B&O. It has always seemed as though the B&O was a "railroader's railroad": it had single and multiple track main lines, locomotives generally familiar to those returning from World War I, and a passenger service that made up in style what it lacked in speed.

The B&O enjoys an impressive list of firsts, but most significant of all is the technological pioneering involved in thrusting itself across a tumultuous sea of mountains with only an intuitive belief that it was at all possible. This gigantic undertaking would be done with steam power, and this book pictures the ultimate triumph of steam locomotion in conquering the harsh terrain.

Sharp curves characterized the route between Baltimore and Harpers Ferry, and from there the line struck out cross-country before rejoining the Potomac River a few miles beyond Martinsburg, West Virginia.

Not until November of 1842 did the B&O reach Cumberland, Maryland, the important commercial center which called itself the Queen City of the Alleghenies. Fortunately for the B&O, Cumberland had become a major source of traffic as the area's coal and iron industries began shipping their products east. The railroad was chronically short of cash and needed every penny of revenue it could find as it gathered its resources for the great assault on the Alleghenies.

After reaching Piedmont, West Virginia in 1851, the road literally threw itself against the mountains by scaling the first barrier with seventeen long miles at the prescribed grade limit of 2.2%. At 2628 feet, the summit at Altamont was, and is, the highest main line crossing of the Alleghenies. After Altamont, the line dipped down through Oakland, only to face another summit at Terra Alta, West Virginia. The line then dropped more than 1100 feet down twisting Cranberry grade to the little town of Rowlesburg located on the Cheat River.

Still challenged by the mountains, engineer Latrobe took his men up the side of the Cheat River Valley and out across the ridge, reaching the final summit at Kingwood Tunnel. From there, it was down again to the Tygart River Valley and the town of Grafton, West Virginia.

At Grafton, the railroad split, one route heading diagonally north and west to the Ohio River at Wheeling, the other heading due west for Parkersburg some ninety miles farther south along the river.

Although the B&O had reached the Ohio River in late 1852, it became commercially imperative to gain access to the rich, rapidly expanding Pittsburgh market. However, a straightforward, competitive invasion of what the Pennsylvania Railroad considered its private turf was next to impossible. The answer to the B&O's need appeared in the form of the struggling Pittsburgh & Connellsville Railroad which was building southeast toward Connellsville, Meyersdale, and the Maryland state line. By advancing funds to the P&C in exchange for increasing control, the B&O eventually got the road built into Cumberland in May of 1871. The P&C lost its visual identity forever in 1884 when its equipment was included in the B&O's systemwide renumbering.

The link to Pittsburgh left Cumberland by following the broad valley of Wills Creek northward into Pennsylvania. At Hyndman, the creek and railroad turned west and the rails commenced their assault on the mountains. The higher the line got, the stiffer the grade became until it topped out at 2½% between Mance and Manila. A tunnel, almost a mile long, penetrated the shoulder of the mountain and the line emerged at the crest of the hill, 2258 feet above sea level. They called the summit Sand Patch, and this name was given to the some twenty miles of mountain railroad the men and their trains would face.

Once over the top at Sand Patch, it was downhill all the way. The railroad followed the Casselman River to Confluence where the waters joined the Youghiogheny River and the rails tagged along for the balance of the run to Connellsville.

This look at the B&O depicts the road's struggle to master the Alleghenies. The time will be the final years of steam power in all its fulminating glory. The coverage will begin with the East End of the Cumberland Division, for this is the prelude to the battles with the mountains. After a brief pause at Cumberland, the scene shifts to the West End of the division, famous for its Seventeen Mile, Cranberry, Cheat River, and Newburg grades plus the action at Terra Alta and M&K Junction. Then the camera returns to Cumberland for the assault on Sand Patch made by the line through Connellsville to Pittsburgh. It was on these two routes that big steam going all out delivered its *Thunder in the Alleghenies*.

CONTENTS

FRONT COVER:
B&O excellence in motive power and maintenance of way are evident in this classic view at Mance in the bright sunshine of April 29, 1955. The hills reverberate to the thunder of No. 7606. — *Color photo by Robert F. Collins.*

INSIDE FRONT COVER:
A merchandise train for Connellsville and points west clears the tunnel on the crest of the Alleghenies at Sand Patch on April 5, 1947. One of the B&O's brawny 2–10–0's heads the consist onto the downgrade. The twin-spout tank serves the main and a connection with the Western Maryland Railway. — *Wm. Price.*

LEFT:
Night and day, the B&O's giants waited for assignments on the steep grades they had been built to conquer. Steam up, this nighttime view at the ready tracks was taken June 30, 1956 as the steam age itself was being surrounded by total darkness. — *J. Shaughnessy*

THE CUMBERLAND DIVISION'S EAST END

TECHNICALLY, THE Cumberland Division begins at Weverton, Maryland, about three miles east of Harpers Ferry. But for all practical purposes, the division really begins another three miles east at Brunswick. The B&O created Brunswick, with its big classification yard and engine terminal, to relieve smaller facilities at Martinsburg, West Virginia. For many years, Brunswick has been a classic railroad company town. Westbound trains feed into Brunswick from Point of Rocks where the Metropolitan Branch from Washington joins the Old Main Line from Baltimore. Crews change right beneath the big railroad YMCA, cars are shuffled in or out as necessary, and trains head on out for Cumberland. The eastbound main track passes around the far side of the yard where many eastbound freights are reclassified for movement to Baltimore or Washington. In the eastbound direction, crews change in front of a small passenger shelter.

Leaving Brunswick, westbound trains swing around the big curve at Knoxville, through the interlocking plant at Weverton and onto the Cumberland Division proper. This is also the point at which the Washington County Branch swings off to the north for its bucolic ramble to Hagerstown. The main line passes Sandy Hook, scene of the famous photo showing a B&O passenger train passing a Chesapeake & Ohio Canal barge, and crosses the Potomac into West Virginia at Harpers Ferry. Just beyond this historic town, the railroad leaves the Potomac shoreline and cuts cross-country through rolling farmland to Martinsburg. Much of the terminal area here appears little changed from Civil War days, even to the pair of beehive-shaped roundhouses.

Between Hedgesville and Cherry Run, where the line rejoins the Potomac River, the B&O encounters North Mountain. This is the first roll in the terrain that is part of the Alleghenies. The original track alignment went across the ridge, approached by short grades on either side. During the World War I era, a low-gradient line built around the end of the ridge along the Potomac eliminated the need to station helper engines at Cherry Run. A principal connection with the Western Maryland Railway main line is made at Cherry Run. Run-through freights destined for the Reading Railroad cross over to the WM here and climb Williamsport Hill to Hagerstown. It was on this grade that the unforgettable teams of B&O EM–1 articulated and WM I–2 heavy Decapod steam locomotives slugged it out with coal loads for the New York market.

The railroad hugs the south bank of the Potomac from Cherry Run to North Branch — within whistling distance of Cumberland. The old main line track kept to the river with what seemed like a never-ending procession of sweeping curves. The exception was at Doe Gully where a tunnel was drilled to cut off a large kink in the river. The single-track bore became a real operating bottleneck until it was daylighted and double-tracked after the turn of the century.

As traffic increased in the early twentieth century, operations on this section of the line became clogged repeatedly. Dan Willard, who became president of the B&O in 1910, was persuaded that the best solution to this problem was to provide freight traffic with its own route. The result was the Magnolia Cutoff, a double-track railroad that avoided hundreds of degrees of curvature, some choppy profile, and shortened the trip by five miles between Paw Paw and Doe Gully. Completed during the World War I period, the Cutoff served freight traffic while passenger traffic continued to flow through the Potomac valley scenery on the old line.

Continuing west, Green Spring, site of a tie-treating plant, is reached. This is the junction point for the South Branch Subdivision, a 52-mile branch to Moorefield and Petersburg which survives on a diet of agricultural products and coal for the West Virginia School for the Deaf at Romney. Ex-Buffalo & Susquehanna 2–8–0's paraded through the cornfields and past the chicken brooders along the branch.

After Green Spring comes Patterson Creek, junction point for another cutoff. The double-track Patterson Creek Cutoff bypasses Cumberland by diverging here and rejoining the main line to Grafton at McKenzie, nine miles west of Cumberland. Coal traffic traveling the cutoff from the west not only avoided the yard and terminal congestion in Cumberland but also saved a distance of ten miles. The division's crack passenger train, the *Cincinnatian*, running on a daylight schedule from Baltimore to

Cincinnati, used the Patterson Creek Cutoff to save as much time as possible in covering the B&O's jagged profile.

The main line route from Patterson Creek re-enters Maryland at North Branch for its approach to the city of Cumberland. Passengers sometimes alighted to take a breath of air beneath the facade of the staid Queen City station-hotel, a Cumberland landmark since 1872. Until 1942, the Cumberland & Pennsylvania Railroad's Tuscan red gas car visited the B&O station daily on its three round trips into the nearby Allegany County hills.

Cumberland is the operating heart of the Cumberland Division. The huge hump yard, also on the east side of town, handles the flow of freight traffic funneled in from the west. Motive power is changed as needed for the transition from the river valley running of the East End to the mountain climbing on the West End and on the line to Pittsburgh. To service the array of motive power, Cumberland's shop facilities were second only to the big shops at Mt. Clare in Baltimore.

W. Hopkins

The Brunswick roundhouse forms the backdrop for No. 659 as it works some hoppers into the east end classification yard on May 23, 1953. The engine is one of sixty-four L–2b switchers that were converted from E–27 2–8–0's between 1926 and 1929.

W. Hopkins

LEFT:
Steam was still abundant in the Brunswick servicing area in 1953, although all steam assignments would soon be moved to the lines west of Cumberland. Big Six No. 6160 trades pleasantries with a brace of brand-new F-units.

OPPOSITE:
In common with most other large roads, the B&O tried various models offered by the major locomotive manufacturers. A trio of road switchers from (right to left) Fairbanks-Morse, Baldwin, and General Motors' Electro-Motive Division line up at Brunswick engine terminal. The road numbers are 927, 899, and 721 respectively.

T. F. Gleichmann, Jr.

W. Hopkins

T. F. Gleichmann, Jr.

THIS PAGE, TOP:

The fog of December 6, 1952's morning hasn't quite lifted as No. 4241 swings off the main line onto the Washington County branch at Weverton. This point marks the official start of the Cumberland Division. The Chessie merger made this branch to Hagerstown superfluous and it was abandoned in 1978.

THIS PAGE, BOTTOM:

Martinsburg's two enclosed roundhouses date from the nineteenth century. No. 4423, a Q–4, gets a little Alemite treatment shortly after Independence Day, 1954.

OPPOSITE:

Eastbound No. 7610 approaches the base of Williamsport Hill on Western Maryland tracks. In a matter of minutes, WM's No.1120 will ease up to the bay window caboose now hidden around the curve and the best power of two roads will put on a real show up the hill to Hagerstown.

Wm. Price

7616
7616

Wm. Price

THIS PAGE:
Length and strength were two words that surely applied to the B&O. An articulated EM–1 — this is No. 7603 — extends itself across the solid stonework over Cacapan River en route to Brunswick.

OPPOSITE PAGE, TOP:
Work on the Berkeley Springs branch was handed to No. 3130 in March of 1952. Seen at Hancock station, across the Potomac from the Maryland town, this 1907 Pittsburgh product was built as Buffalo & Susquehanna No. 154. The unusual feature of inboard cylinder valves was retained to the end.

OPPOSITE PAGE, BOTTOM:
No. 6112 has just cleared the signal bridge at Hancock. With only 31 cars on the drawbar and no fight against gravity, the engine is barely working and the fireman gets to take a look at what's happening on the engineer's side of the cab.

Both, R. F. Collins

R. F. Collins

[ABOVE:] **In September of 1949, semaphores were being replaced with color position lights on the East End. A 14-car mail and express train makes good time at Orleans Road interlocking with No. 5000, a P–1c, in the lead.** [BELOW:] **A brace of Alco FA's heads west onto the Magnolia Cutoff, having passed through the cut that marks the location of the old tunnel at Doe Gully. The curving tracks departing at the left belong to the old main line. How are those ballast edges for maintaining the right-of-way!**

W. R. Hicks

LEFT:
Westbound near Hansrote, No. 5307 roars west over the old main line with Train #21. The photograph was taken from the embankment of the Magnolia Cutoff which also follows the curve of the river and can be spotted as the high line in the background. The next to last coach on the train is an every other day Erie Railroad car between Cleveland and Washington.

Wm. Price

RIGHT:
When the mountains closed in on the Potomac, concrete retaining walls were needed to buttress the shelf carrying the Magnolia Cutoff. No. 823 leads a matched set of Alco FA's along the West Virginia banks of the Potomac.

W. R. Hicks

Wm. Price

W. R. Hicks

OPPOSITE, LEFT:
At Magnolia, West Virginia, the Cutoff crosses the twisting Potomac into Maryland and dives into Graham Tunnel. A westbound reefer train is seen making this crossing on July 10, 1952.

OPPOSITE, RIGHT:
Another westbound train is seen, this time from the mountain on the Maryland side. The limestone cars extend through a crotch in the hills separating the hairpin turns of the Potomac. Westbound trains on the old main line pass from left to right on the tracks seen on the opposite bank.

THIS PAGE, TOP:
A westbound EM–1 starts across the river at Magnolia in a view at trackside on the old main. Upper quadrant semaphores protected the old main in 1952, while the color light signal on the cutoff can be seen above the tank car.

THIS PAGE, BOTTOM:
The semaphore blade at Magnolia has dropped about halfway as an A–B set of E–6's zip west with Train #11.

Both, Wm. Price

W. R. Hicks

THIS PAGE:
At the other portal of Graham Tunnel, the Cutoff immediately recrosses the Potomac and the old main line which followed the river around the shoulder of the mountain. The *West Virginian,* bound for Cumberland, cants around Kessler's Curve.

OPPOSITE PAGE, TOP:
Graham Tunnel connects the two river crossings in a straight line. Facing away from Kessler's curve, the camera looks east "through the state of Maryland" and back into West Virginia at Magnolia in the daylight beyond.

OPPOSITE PAGE, BOTTOM:
A couple of twists of the river later, the Magnolia Cutoff emerges from Carothers Tunnel to run side-by-side again with the old main line. President-class Pacific No. 5313 handled Train #21 on March 16, 1952.

W. R. Hicks

R. F. Collins

W. R. Hicks

Wm. Price

[ABOVE:] **The Magnolia Cutoff merges with the old main line at Paw Paw, having saved 5.8 miles and hundreds of degrees of curvature. A two-unit set of F's gets a clear indication at signal bridge 156/41.** [LEFT:] **The semaphore bridge at Patterson Creek's westbound approach signal witnessed endless strings of 50-ton hoppers. A 2–10–2 marches by, railroading the B&O way.**

[RIGHT:] **Flying pumps herald the passage of No. 7701 just east of Patterson Creek in April of 1951. Ten of these class KB–1 2–6–6–4's were bought from the Seaboard in 1947 to overcome a postwar power shortage. With 69″ drivers, they were fast, smooth, and easy-steaming.** [BELOW:] **No. 7703, also near Patterson Creek, has had its front end cleaned up by relocation of the air pumps to the pilot deck. Crews really liked these engines and the fireman gives a nice wave to the camera.**

Both, Wm. Price

6123
B&O

OPPOSITE:

No. 6123 works a string of high cars through the interlocking and onto the Patterson Creek Cutoff headed for Keyser. In April of 1947, the class S–1 2–10–2's were standard power for heavy freights on the East End.

THIS PAGE:

A matched set of F–3's brings Train #87's mixed consist of standard and streamlined cars through Patterson Creek on July 10, 1952.

Both, Wm. Price

R. H. Kindig

Wm. Price

W. R. Hicks

OPPOSITE PAGE, TOP:
At 1:37 P.M. on July 29, 1949, a remarkable moment in railfan photography occurred as the passing of Trains #31 and 2nd #8, both running at 50 mph, was recorded from the bluff high above the Patterson Creek tower.

OPPOSITE PAGE, BOTTOM LEFT:
The elegant *Cincinnatian* rolls off the Patterson Creek Cutoff, having bypassed Cumberland. This premier train also used the Magnolia Cutoff in an all-out effort to minimize travel time between Baltimore and Cincinnati. The train, which entered revenue service on January 19, 1947, is seen here on April 26 during its first year of service. The trainsets were rebuilt from heavyweight equipment at the Mt. Clare shops. Cafe-observation No. 3304, the *Peebles Corner,* brings up the rear on this eastbound run.

OPPOSITE PAGE, BOTTOM RIGHT:
Since the *Capitol Limited* did serve Cumberland, E–6 No. 63 curves to its right, remaining on the westbound main at Patterson Creek.

THIS PAGE, TOP:
Hot-shot freights got lots of power. With the Alco FA's churning away and the EM–1 really boiling, the heavy tonnage truly rolled through Patterson Creek on April 5, 1951.

THIS PAGE, BOTTOM:
In work train service, No. 1474 pauses east of Cumberland. The engine has forty-four years of service, having been built in 1903 when the B&O was under Pennsy control. Originally used as main line passenger power, the engine was constructed with a Belpaire firebox, hallmark of the PRR.

Wm. Price

Wm. Price

RIGHT:

A brace of FA's burble through Mexico Farm in September of 1951 with a reefer block. The Alcos were impressive in B&O's blue, gray, and black livery set off by the capitol dome.

Wm. Price

Wm. Price

LEFT:

Two-year old No. 7620 wheels the merchandise toward the Cumberland yard in April, 1947.

Wm. Price

LEFT:
Train #21 heads west on the homestretch into Cumberland. No. 5305, the former *President Jackson,* was a class P-7c Pacific.

RIGHT:
This was the Cumberland Rolling Mill where scrap iron from around the system was brought, melted down, and reprocessed into structural shapes such as car side ribs and signal bridge members. The complex was torn down during the 1970s.

Broadway Limited Collection

Both, Wm. Price

[ABOVE:] **Halfway through a Class 3 overhaul of No. 7629 in June of 1958, the decision was made in Baltimore to incur no major expense on steam locomotives since they would soon be scrapped. Artist John Wenrich works intently to capture his subject, while a Big Six, shorn of its cab, awaits the same fate as the EM–1.** [BELOW:] **The beautiful Queen City station-hotel was a Cumberland landmark for a hundred years.**

Wm. Price

The first of the finest poses at Cumberland's station. Since this picture was taken in September of 1956 and EM–1's hadn't been worked in passenger service since 1947, the occasion is marked as being a fan trip.

THE CUMBERLAND DIVISION'S WEST END

UPON LEAVING THE Queen City station for Grafton, trains rattle through the switchwork of Viaduct Junction and swing across Wills Creek and the WM on a long concrete arch viaduct. The viaduct was built of brick as a single track structure before the Civil War and substantially rebuilt with double tracks in the early 1900s. After passing through a deep cut, the tracks rejoin the Potomac River. The upper valley of the Potomac is broad with gentle hills, allowing trains to get a good roll on before the rigors ahead. The WM line to Elkins parallels the B&O between Cumberland and Bloomington, crossing back and forth between Maryland and West Virginia several times. At a point known as Twenty-first Bridge, the B&O crosses the Potomac and enters Keyser, West Virginia. Keyser's large coal marshalling yard was established when the yards at Cumberland were bypassed by the Patterson Creek Cutoff. A large engine terminal and car shop are also located at Keyser.

West of the yards, the hills close in again, bringing the railroad back to the banks of the Potomac. The towns of Piedmont, Luke, Westernport, and Bloomington seemingly run together along both sides of the river, with the West Virginia Pulp & Paper Company's mill dominating the area. Piedmont is the helper terminal and feeder point for shipments from the Georges Creek coal fields. Past Luke, the B&O returns to Maryland as it crosses the Bloomington Viaduct over the Potomac. It is here that Seventeen Mile Grade begins.

Passenger trains doubleheaded the hill with a Q–4 class Mike tacked on ahead of the usual P–1d Pacific. Freight trains required immense power, making this the land of giants on the B&O. Articulated steam power was first built for the B&O in 1904. Old Maude, as this first Mallet was called, had an 0–6–6–0 wheel arrangement that did not track well. She did, however, lead the way to the 2–8–8–0's in class EL and, ultimately, to the B&O's finest, the 2–8–8–4's of class EM–1. Freights cross the viaduct at the foot of the grade making about forty miles an hour. Train speed decreases as the EL- or EM-class engine on the head end struggles up the hill until the rear end helpers catch up to the train and begin to push mightily. Train speeds generally decrease to about ten miles an hour by then. The rear end help usually consists of a pair of articulateds.

A wye and water station mark the summit of the hill at Altamont where the helpers cut off for the roll back down to Piedmont. Traveling west, the railroad sags a little as it passes through the mountain resort towns of Deer Park, Mountain Lake Park, and Oakland. Most well-known of these towns is Deer Park, for this is the source of the pure water which is bottled commercially and was to be seen gracing the tables of the B&O's dining car service.

A short grade brings the line to Terra Alta, crest of the hard eastbound climb out of the Cheat River basin. "CA" Tower is the center of action here as eastbound helpers are cut off and returned with the flow of westbound traffic down the hill.

The descent is made on Cranberry Grade. Although not as long as Seventeen Mile Grade, Cranberry is almost as steep and is highlighted by the sweeping Salt Lick Curve. The foot of Cranberry Grade is marked by M&K Junction. M&K stands for Morgantown & Kingwood, an early line acquired by the B&O.

The operating significance of this point deep in the valley of the Cheat River is the engine terminal to service and dispatch the helpers working east up Cranberry Grade and west out of the valley up Cheat River Grade. A scattering of houses and stores called Rowlesburg lies across the river from the engine terminal. There can be little doubt as to the town's reason for being. Even the front door of the New Howard Hotel is only twenty steps from the station platform.

Cheat River Grade begins at the west end of the yard and the helpers are already going down on their knees as they rattle the windows on the little depot. On the climb, a large amount of masonry work can be seen holding the railroad up against the side of the hill. The stonework culminates with the impressive Tray Run viaduct. This stone arch construction was performed at the turn of the century to replace an iron structure originally used at this point.

The railroad reaches its next major summit at Tunnelton, where it connects with the West Virginia Northern, a short line. Westbound trains then dive through Kingwood Tunnel and

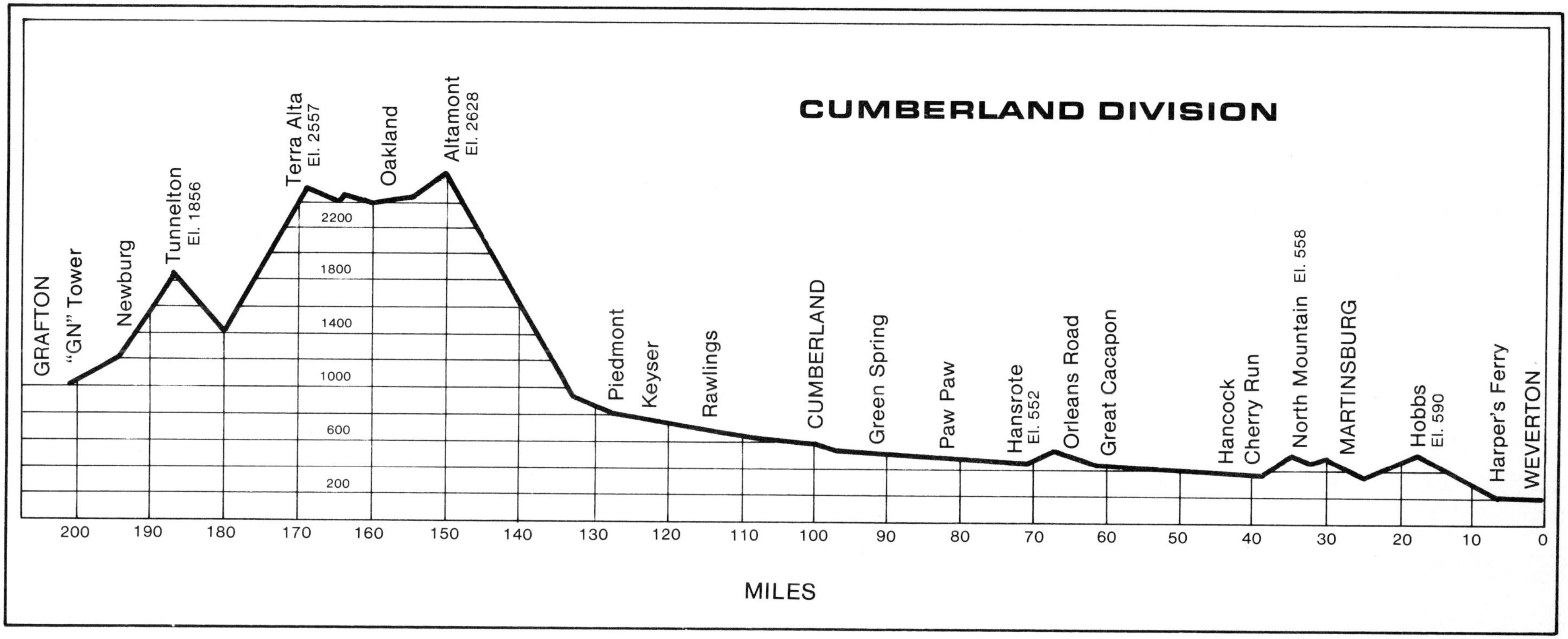

wind along Racoon and Three Forks Creek as they descend Newburg Grade. Finally, the railroad arrives at what passes for a water level route into Grafton.

Grafton exudes railroading. The entire valley seems filled by yards and the engine terminal. The scene from the footbridge over the tracks is one of smoky splendor. The roof of the roundhouse supports part of the bridge, and trains bound for Wheeling and Parkersburg roll beneath one's feet. The west end of the yard is bracketed by the towering coal dock and the neo-classical passenger station. Here the big power needed on the mountains relinquish their tonnage to smaller road power. Likely as not, a Q–4b Mike would head out for Parkersburg with the same train brought in by an EM–1 articulated. Low-drivered P–1d Pacifics, standard passenger power on the West End, are replaced at Grafton by speedier P–5's or P–6's for the continuing trips west.

Diesel locomotives put in an early appearance on the West End. Since this is the B&O's biggest operating challenge, it gave the newcomers a good test. So well did these strange horses from General Motors' stable perform, that steam on the West End soon became a fragrant memory.

5003
5003

OPPOSITE:
En route to Grafton, No. 5003 crosses the concrete viaduct in Cumberland with Train #11. Except for the bulbous Farina-styled postwar Nash in the background, this 1949 picture could just as well have been taken ten to fifteen years earlier.

THIS PAGE, TOP:
At McKenzie, nine miles west of Cumberland, the Patterson Creek Cutoff rejoins the main line. A westbound Shriner's special, completing its run over the Cutoff, passes an eastbound coal drag just entering the Cutoff. The crew of No. 7101, which holds the westbound main from Cumberland, takes some air and sees the sights.

THIS PAGE, BOTTOM:
Before being cleared to continue west, No. 7101 witnesses the eastbound passage of the *Cincinnatian* as it too takes the Patterson Creek Cutoff.

All, Wm. Price

THIS PAGE:
EM–1 No. 7604 heels to the curve across Twenty-first Bridge. The coal drag is eastbound as it crosses the Potomac in March, 1952.

OPPOSITE PAGE, TOP:
In an opposite direction view at Twenty-first Bridge, westbound F–units power Train #29 under the Western Maryland's truss, over the waters, and on into West Virginia.

OPPOSITE PAGE, BOTTOM:
No. 5579 is seen from the WM truss bridge with the mostly mail and express consist of Train #30, the eastbound counterpart to Train #29. The date is April 28, 1955 and use of the class T–2 Mountain types had become rare on the West End.

Wm. Price

Wm. Price

R. F. Collins

[OPPOSITE:] **An abundance of steam power was to be found at Keyser in the spring of 1952 and an EM–1 can be seen rolling up the lead from the roundhouse. The car shops are going full blast and the sorting of coal loads keeps the switchers busy.** [RIGHT:] **In a work scene at Piedmont, Q–4 No. 4412 ties onto the rear markers for the all-out push up Seventeen Mile Grade. With only one Mike as a pusher, this must be a lighter than average train.** [BELOW:] **Typical of operations on Seventeen Mile Grade in the days when passenger business was brisk, No. 4417 hammers uphill ahead of No. 5086, a Pacific that was serving as the road power. It was a scene to be observed many times daily.**

Wm. Price

Wm. Price

R. F. Collins

LEFT:
Another endless string of loaded hoppers drifts through Swanton, Maryland. The hard labor for No. 7608 is over for this trip, but keeping the rolling tonnage in check down Seventeen Mile Grade requires a steady hand on the air by the engineer.

Both, R. H. Kindig

RIGHT:
The bullet-nosed P-7 normally assigned to the *Cincinnatian* broke a spring hanger at Keyser on September 29, 1948. Suddenly, Q-4 No. 4416 became the star of the show and, in a Cinderella-like role, headed west toward the summit at Altamont.

The versatility of Q–4's was proven time and again as they worked passenger and freight, on the point or pushing from the rear. Here, No. 4405 leads Train #11 through a reverse curve on Seventeen Mile Grade.

Wm. Price

Wm. Price

R. H. Kindig

LEFT:
The operating department didn't spare the horses in getting "Timesaver Service" over the Alleghenies. No. 931 leads two three-unit sets of blue and gray over the summit at Altamont on a bright fall day in 1953. The helper wye in the background would become superfluous within the next few years.

BELOW:
In a classic view at the summit, EM–1 No. 7610 eases carefully onto the eastbound downgrade with fifty-one cars of tide coal headed for Keyser at 8:43 A.M. on September 28, 1948.

OPPOSITE:
The *Cincinnatian* splits the quiet air of Mountain Lake Park as it speeds westward across the mountain plateau. It is late June of 1950, and the train should have no trouble in maximizing its trip mileage in the daylight hours.

Wm. Price

PARK

D. Duke

D. Duke

LEFT:

Oakland was a scheduled stop for Train #11. No. 5035, a P–1d, was standard passenger power on the West End. The class was created at Mt. Clare from old Q–1 boilers and running gear from early P and P-1 engines.

BELOW:

Having gotten its load of black diamonds over the crest at Terra Alta, No. 7213 rolls eastward through Corinth, West Virginia at 45 mph.

RIGHT:
Nos. 7169 and 7605 bring sixty-nine empty hoppers into Terra Alta. No. 7169 is an EL–5a, originally built as a USRA standard Mallet in 1920. Like most of its class, the engine was rebuilt as a simple articulated by 1930 and will continue on this run down Cranberry Grade to M&K Junction where it will rejoin the helper pool.

BELOW:
This is Salt Lick Curve on Cranberry Grade. The sand-whitened tracks in the foreground are evidence of the heavy eastbound grade which, with a length of twelve miles, is almost as steep as Seventeen Mile Grade is to reach the plateau in the westbound direction.

R. H. Kindig

R. H. Kindig

D. Duke

R. H. Kindig

ABOVE:
With twelve cars, its all-out for Nos. 4407 and 5052 to maintain a 35 mph speed up Cranberry Grade and around Salt Lick Curve. This is Train #30, operated primarily for mail and express bound for Baltimore and Washington.

LEFT:
No. 5304 climbs Cranberry Grade in June of 1949 with the *Cincinnatian*. Underneath the shiny blue shrouding is the *President Monroe*, a P–7 Pacific.

R. H. Kindig

LEFT:
Curving back through Rodemer, West Virginia, No. 7032 rolls toward M&K Junction to aid the next freight east. The old Mallet was built as an 0–8–8–0 of class LL–1 — with no stokers! The only changes since 1913 are the added pony truck, a shortened cab, and stokers. In this September 1948 view, the locomotive had less than two years of service left.

RIGHT:
This action scene of heavy B&O power took place at Amblersburg, halfway up Cranberry Grade. EM–1 No. 7602 on track 2 overtakes a pair of EL-class helpers shoving hard on Track 3. The view is from the cab of the lead helper. In about 30 minutes, the operator at Terra Alta is going to be one busy gentleman.

W. R. Hicks

Both, R. H. Kindig

ABOVE:
The never-ending parade up Cranberry Grade continues at Amblersburg with Nos. 7133 and 7047 at work on the rear, the latter still retaining its configuration as a Mallet compound.

LEFT:
A bright July morning sun lights up EM–1 No.7621 as it wakes up McMillan, West Virginia. There can be no doubt that this eastbound train of coal loads has a pair of helpers blasting away on the rear.

R. H. Kindig

ABOVE:
The foot of the long eastbound climb up Cranberry Grade is at M&K Junction. Old EL–4 No. 7032 and EL–1a cannonade the skies at the rear of yet another endless string of loaded hoppers on July 26, 1949.

RIGHT:
Baldwin demonstrator No. 6000 sits next to the enginehouse at M&K Junction on May 28, 1948 between trials in helper service. Although the B&O bought Baldwins, none were of the Centipede design.

W. R. Hicks

R. H. Kindig

LEFT:
After a brief pause at M&K Junction, No. 7170 gets its string of seventy-seven empties rolling westbound across the Cheat River and into Rowlesburg. Cheat River Grade begins right here.

BELOW:
A rockfall has blocked the eastbound track in June of 1949, necessitating use of the wrong main by Q–4 No. 4481. A temporary signal has been installed to control this stretch of what has become a single track railroad for the time being. The Cheat River Valley lies in the summer haze beyond.

R. H. Kindig

R. H. Kindig

R. H. Kindig

D. Duke

[ABOVE:] **A stone viaduct and an EM–1 — both symbolic of B&O strength — are seen at Tray Run on July 26, 1949. No. 7609 descends with a mixed bag of sixty-five cars well in hand.** [TOP RIGHT:] **No. 5301 hammers across Tray Run at 30 mph as it lifts the five-car *Cincinnatian* out of the Cheat River Valley.** [BOTTOM RIGHT:] **"K" Tower is at Blaser, West Virginia, about a mile and a half away from the summit at Kingwood Tunnel. Train #11 continues the climb as a Q-4 in the background prepares for its reverse movement to M&K Junction.**

R. H. Kindig

[LEFT:] **Smoke from a pair of EL's darkens the West Virginia skies as another long shove to Tunnelton nears its end on July 27, 1949.** [BELOW:] **No. 7133, an EL-3a, definitely has an unbuttoned look around the headlight as it awaits the passage of a coal train at Tunnelton. The helper set awaits clearance to either back down to M&K Junction and work Cheat River Grade again or proceed through the tunnel and on down to Grafton to work back up Newburg Grade.** [OPPOSITE PAGE:] **Tunnelton enjoyed a substantial brick depot, somewhat out of keeping with its small mining town character. With a trainload of black diamonds on the drawhead, No. 7623 passes between the depot and the interchange track with the West Virginia Northern.**

Wm. Price

Wm. Price

7623
B&O
7623

Both, R. H. Kindig

[ABOVE:] **The reason for Tunnelton's name is obvious. The original main continues in service using the single-track bore. The Willard-era improvement program ended a traffic bottleneck that had developed by adding a double-track tunnel at a slightly lower elevation. No. 7154 emerges from the east portal with a coal extra.** [LEFT:] **Helpers 7041 and 7102 clear Kingwood tunnel and enter town, their long push up Newburg grade successfully completed.**

D. Duke

From a vantage point above the portal, the camera catches a glimpse of the westbound *Cincinnatian* following the original route into its tunnel.

[OPPOSITE PAGE:] **No. 7616 rounds the reverse curve at Austen, three miles west of Tunnelton. It was muggy on July 27, 1949 as indicated by the condensation caused by the cool water in the lower half of the tender. This is evidence of an EM–1's reserve capacity when working Newburg Grade.** [RIGHT:] **Nos. 7109 and 7205 bring up the rear of 7616's train. The caboose is No. C2500, B&O's first bay window hack. Built in 1931 at Mt. Clare, it was an experimental design that proved to be successful.**

All, R. H. Kindig

LEFT:
EM-1 No. 7609 blasts upgrade toward Tunnelton as a pair of helpers drifts by on return to Grafton. The siding in the foreground is the interchange track with the Premar Coal Company which worked its trackage with a little Shay.

P. R. Hastings

P. R. Hastings

LEFT:
Grafton, terminus of the Cumberland Division's West End, was a bit coal smudged in May of 1953. This view looks east across the yards to the passenger station on the left and the coal dock on the right. No. 5068 waits to bark out of town with a westbound passenger extra.

ABOVE:
The granite-faced facade of the Grafton station looms over a platform filled with the classic impedimentia — milk cans, mail sacks, cartons of express and some lucky lad's new bicycle.

W. Hopkins

W. Hopkins

[ABOVE LEFT:] **A string of company hoppers trail Q–3 No. 4576 past the Grafton station platform in July, 1954. Most likely, the empties are headed down the old Coal & Coke line to Richwood or Charleston.** [ABOVE RIGHT:] **Class P–1c and P–1d Pacifics worked the West End's passenger service over the mountains out of Grafton. No. 5005, refueled for an eastbound run, is seen in July of 1954. By 1957, these workhorses had all been scrapped.** [RIGHT:] **P–7d No. 5317, subbing for a streamlined sister, brings the eastbound** ***Cincinnatian*** **across the Tygart River into Grafton and onto the Cumberland Division.**

R. H. Kindig

THE PITTSBURGH DIVISION OVER SAND PATCH

THE EASTERN END of the Pittsburgh Division extends from Cumberland, Maryland to Connellsville, Pennsylvania. Trains on the Pittsburgh Division leave the Queen City station, roll straight through the switchwork at Viaduct Junction and right onto somebody else's railroad. Trackage from Viaduct Junction to Mt. Savage Junction is owned by the Cumberland & Pennsylvania Railroad whose predecessors built through the Cumberland Narrows in the 1840s. The B&O has, however, leased and maintained this section since the 1870s.

The Narrows has always been a strategic avenue of transportation. In its history, the thousand foot deep gash in Haystack Mountain has been occupied by an Indian footpath, the original National Road (now US 40), the Georges Creek & Cumberland Railroad, the Pennsylvania Railroad in Maryland, the Cumberland & Pennsylvania Railroad, the Baltimore & Ohio Railroad, the Cumberland Electric, and the Cumberland & Westernport Electric Railway, plus the Pennsylvania Railroad via trackage rights. And also in that gash is Wills Creek which occasionally goes out of its banks with unfortunate results for some if not all of the other occupants of the narrow defile. In the 1930s, the trolley lines were abandoned and, by the 1940s, the Western Maryland had absorbed all of the short lines, with the result that it shared the track with the B&O between Cumberland and Mt. Savage Junction.

At Mt. Savage Junction, B&O trains roll onto their own rails for the balance of the run over Sand Patch Grade to Connellsville, Pittsburgh, and beyond. An easy roll up the Wills Creek valley brings the trains to Hyndman, Pennsylvania where the action begins in earnest. The roadman pulls his train up past "Q" Tower, the operator sets the crossovers, and two S–1 2–10–2's ease up to the end sill of the caboose. They whistle off, and more than a quarter million pounds of tractive effort begins to fight eternal gravity. Meanwhile, another pair of helpers waters up and moves into place, waiting to repeat the performance.

It's twenty miles from the tower at Hyndman to the crest of the grade which is located inside Sand Patch Tunnel, and it's uphill all the way. The lower half of the hill, up through Fairhope and Falls Cut Tunnel, hovers around two percent, but the many twisting curves along Wills Creek add to the difficulty. Swinging around the wide horseshoe curve at Mance, things get serious. The hill finally tops out around 2½% at Manila.

The operator at "SA" Tower, located at the west end of Sand Patch Tunnel, has few idle moments since he must keep east and westbound trains and their helpers all sorted out. Eastbound trains usually pick up a helper at Garrett for the last nine miles of their climb to "SA."

Going down the other side, the line ducks under the WM's Keystone Viaduct, through Meyersdale, and under the impressive steel trestle that is the WM's Salisbury Viaduct. The remaining run down the Casselman and Youghiogheny River Valleys into Connellsville is easy operation and scenic as well.

Depending on tonnage, eastbound trains may rate a helper out of Connellsville. In earlier years, Rockwood, forty-three miles east of Connellsville, was the primary eastbound helper station. Later on, helpers would work east from Connellsville to Sand Patch, then back down to the pocket track at Garrett to wait further service.

For many years, the Pittsburgh Division was dominated by the S–1 class Big Six 2–10–2's. Four-cylinder articulated power was intermittently used on Sand Patch until diesels began displacing the big steam power off the West End. The 6000-series, from which the term *Big Sixes* was derived, were big brutes, but with their 64-inch drivers (58 inches on class S) they could also run like a Mike. For a time, a Big Six would occasionally lead a shiny new E–6 diesel to boost the *Capitol Limited* over the hill.

While the 6000's were perhaps the stars of the Pittsburgh Division, a wide variety of B&O power polished these rails. For years, the *Capitol Limited* departed Cumberland for Pittsburgh with a T–2 4–8–2 on the point. War baby T–3's put in an all-too-brief but memorable appearance before most were banished to the flatlands of Indiana. Even the ex-Boston & Maine 4–8–2's made a token appearance before suffering the same fate as the T–3's. And finally, the EL 2–8–8–0's and EM–1 2–8–8–4's helped write the final chapter of steam on Sand Patch.

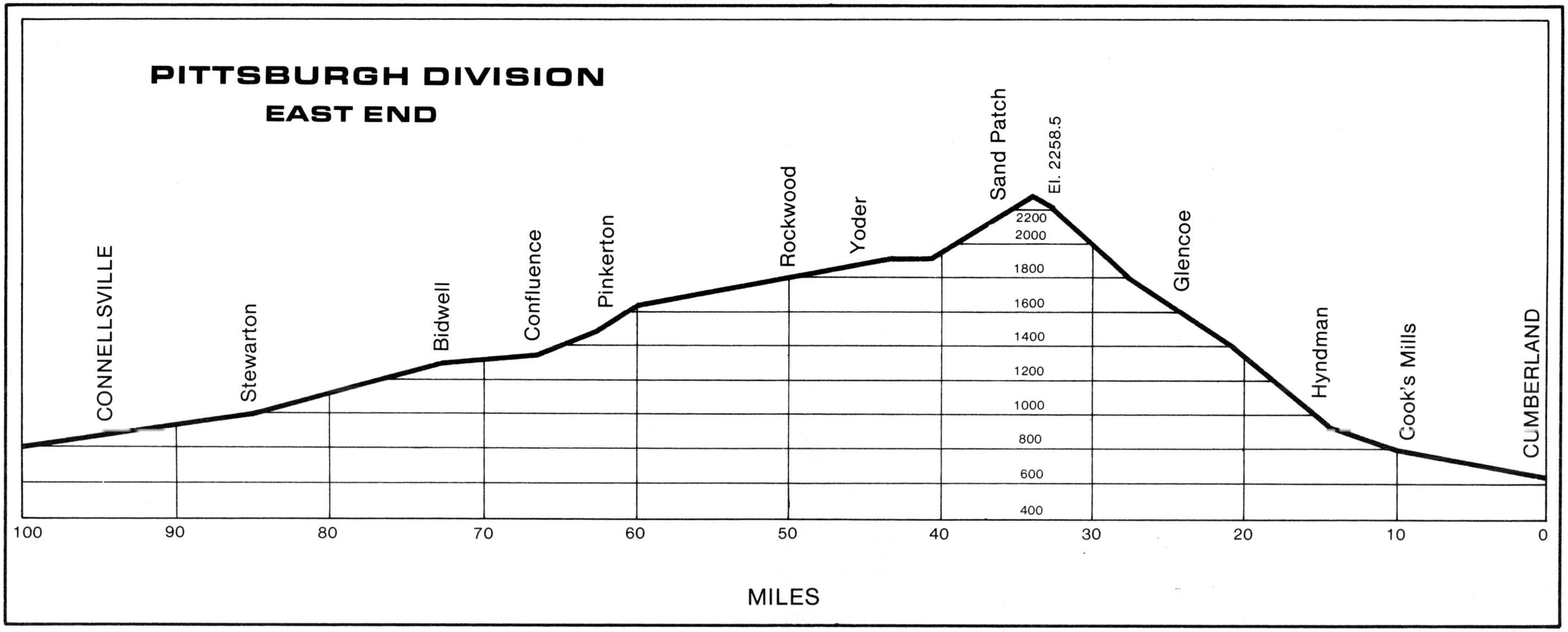

Prior to facing the rigors of the mountains west of Cumberland, B&O's massive steam power was routinely scrutinized by engine inspectors in search of incipient flaws or maladjustments that would lead to road failures.

J. Shaughnessy

RADIATOR
SERVICE
6200

OPPOSITE PAGE:
No. 6200 rolls a string of empties through Viaduct Junction in Cumberland, headed for Connellsville. The main line to Grafton swings off to the right. The date is March 30, 1956 and the sight of a Big Six in service is becoming increasingly rare.

RIGHT:
No. 4740 passes through the Cumberland Narrows on trackage that was operated and maintained by the B&O under lease from the Cumberland & Pennsylvania. The engine also had a non-B&O origin, having been built for the Buffalo, Rochester & Pittsburgh in 1917 and taken onto the B&O roster as class Q–10b when the BR&P was taken over in 1932.

R. F. Collins

Wm. Price

R. F. Collins

LEFT:
Train #9, the *Chicago Express,* wheels through the Narrows behind Mountain-type No. 5510 on June 26, 1941. The locomotive was a water tube firebox experimental model built by Baldwin in 1930.

BELOW:
Late afternoon sun illuminates Train #32 as it breezes through Mt. Savage Junction, the point where the Cumberland & Pennsylvania curves off into the hills and B&O's ownership of its Pittsburgh Division trackage begins. No. 5566 belonged to class T–3, a series of 4–8–2's outshopped at Mt. Clare during World War II using new running gear under old P–1 and Q–1 boilers.

R. F. Collins

Wm. Price

Shiny enough for some publicity work, the B&O's first road freight diesel hauls the merchandise through Mt. Savage Junction on September 19, 1947.

831
831
831
BALTIMORE AND OHIO
859
859

OPPOSITE PAGE:
Diesel power was out in force at Mt. Savage Junction on Independence Day of 1952. A trio of Alco FA's heads for Sand Patch past an idling set of Baldwin Sharks.

TOP RIGHT:
Fifty cars head west with T–3c No. 5591 through Corriganville, Maryland. The track in the foreground is the Cumberland & Pennsylvania's State Line branch.

BOTTOM RIGHT:
A pair of Sharks burbles west through Mt. Savage Junction in March, 1953. The tower in the distance marks the point where eastbound trains leave B&O-owned rails and travel on the C&P through the Narrows.

Wm. Price

R. F. Collins

Wm. Price

Wm. Price

ABOVE:
Just north of Ellerslie, Maryland, a westbound ore train is moved across the Mason-Dixon line into Pennsylvania by mixed motive power from Schenectady and Eddystone. Even more horsepower will tie on at Hyndman for the assault on Sand Patch.

BELOW:
"Q" Tower at Hyndman, Pennsylvania was a busy spot since it was here that helpers were added. A pair of F–7's, slamming through the crossovers used by the helpers, rattles the tower windows with an eastbound "timesaver" freight.

W. Hopkins

BELOW:
B&O experience with diesel power in road service began in the mid-1930s. The vast requirements for complete conversion from steam to diesel took a decade, during which time the products of the major builders were put to the test of time. General Motors' models proved themselves well and although F–7 No. 943 was young when this picture was taken near Hyndman in May of 1952, the B&O had already ordered its first Geeps.

Wm. Price

Wm. Price

ABOVE:
With Big Sixes front and rear, the freight shipments ascend Sand Patch in November, 1954. No. 6168, the lead engine, is one of the class S-1b's that were upgraded with one-piece cast steel engine beds and a front end treatment reminiscent of the P-7d's and P-7e's.

Wm. Price

LEFT:
A string of hoppers gets lifted up the hill near Fairhope as an eastbound disappears in a cloud of coal and brake shoe smoke.

ABOVE:
A pair of Big Sixes leans in hard against the wagon-top caboose and the high cars on Sand Patch. The grade crossing is at Fairhope as seen on June 23, 1954.

Wm. Price

P. R. Hastings

ABOVE:
Falls Cut Tunnel is a short bore through the shoulder of a sidehill. No. 7615 controls a loaded coal train eastbound through the tunnel in June of 1953.

RIGHT:
"FO" Tower — eight miles up from Hyndman and twelve miles down from Sand Patch — provided a degree of operating flexibility on the long grade. A pair of Big Sixes clanks back to Hyndman for another go at the hill.

P. R. Hastings

Wm. Price

OPPOSITE PAGE:
At Southampton, the uphill track looped out to ease the grade. No. 7619, laboring mightily with a westbound freight on February 16, 1956, drew assignments on Sand Patch after diesels bumped the EM-1's off the Cumberland Division.

RIGHT:
Nos. 6116 and 6103 have cut off from their freight in order to maneuver for water at the Southampton tank. The engineer checks his Big Six while the fireboy minds the spout.

P. R. Hastings

Wm. Price

LEFT:
One of the favorite photo locations on Sand Patch was the big horseshoe curve at Mance. A wisp of smoke beyond the first ridge indicates the presence of steam helpers for the pair of F-3's working this westbound "Timesaver" up the hill.

These three pictures illustrate the giant scale on which the B&O operated. From a vantage point about 300 yards upgrade from the road crossing at Mance, the passage of a long merchandise train is seen. No. 7619 passes by on its way up the 2% grade, the sharp, sweeping loop in the background. As the reefers rumble by, the pair of Big Sixes pushing on the rear come into view far across the valley. Minutes later, the rear pushers reach the observer and set up a miniature earthquake of their own.

All, Wm. Price

PACIFIC FRUIT EXPRESS
PFE
43725
REFRIGERATOR
SOUTHERN PACIFIC LINES
NORTH WESTERN
REFRIGERATOR LINE
COMPANY
NWX 612

BALTIMORE & OHIO

Wm. Price

No. 5662 works a string of empty hoppers through Mance in June of 1954. This locomotive was the last in a group of thirteen that were bought in 1947 from the Boston & Maine as the B&M proceeded to dieselize with F–2's instead of waiting for availability of the more powerful model F–3's. The B&O, on the other hand, needed all the big power it could get. Having already created class T–3 4–8–2's at Mt. Clare, the ex-B&M 4–8–2's became class T–4. They gave good service until retired in 1958.

Wm. Price

Because Train #21 made local stops, it had the slowest schedule between Cumberland and Connellsville. None the less, it carried ten cars and needed doubleheading over Sand Patch on April 28, 1953. No. 5003 on the point helps No. 5579, classed a T–3t because it was one of seven T–3's retro-fitted with a huge Vanderbilt tender to extend the operating range.

R. F. Collins

R. F. Collins

TOP LEFT:
No. 6145, with thirty-one years of service, continued to plod up Sand Patch on April 28,1955.

BOTTOM LEFT:
A little less than two miles west of Mance is "GR" Interlocking, better known as Manila, Pennsylvania. This was the steepest part of the grade. Nos. 6195 and 6188, at the head end of ninety-five cars of ore, are just below the tower which handled movements at the east end of Sand Patch Tunnel.

OPPOSITE PAGE:
No. 7120 prepares to dust the tower with cinders on its crawl to the summit. In November of 1949 when this picture was taken, EL class articulateds were rarely seen on a hill dominated by the 2-10-2 Big Sixes.

Wm. Price

GR
TELEVISION

R. F. Collins

THIS PAGE:
No. 6132's helpers have already cut off at the east end of Sand Patch Tunnel. The fifty-two cars of iron ore will pass "SA" Tower at the right and start the downhill run to Rockwood, then head north to the steel mills in Johnstown.

OPPOSITE PAGE, LEFT:
No. 5083 and a sister Pacific lead what looks like Train #21 out of the west portal of Sand Patch Tunnel. A gandy dancer steps out of his shack to monitor the train as it passes.

OPPOSITE PAGE, RIGHT:
Working its way eastbound to Sand Patch, EL-2a No. 7209 braves the gelid Allegheny weather at Keystone in February, 1951.

Wm. Price

Wm. Price

R. F. Collins

LEFT:
The eastbound grade to Sand Patch was neither as long nor as steep as the westbound grade. One Mike at the rear is all that is needed for No. 7136 to get these loads of tide coal up the hill. This view was taken as the train headed under the Western Maryland's Salisbury viaduct on May 19, 1951.

P. R. Hastings

RIGHT:
The valley of the Youghiogheny River reverberates to the bellow of EM-1 No. 7608 as it gets a string of high cars underway at Connellsville in August of 1954.

J. Shaughnessy

ABOVE:
Empty hoppers for the tipples back in the hills pass the neat and trim Connellsville station in 1956. Motive power is No. 5569, itself a neat and trim package turned out by Mt. Clare in 1944.

RIGHT:
The Connellsville engine terminal hosted its traditional Big Six power as well as Baldwin Sharks in 1954. The turntable is located in the background behind the tender.

H. W. Peterson

H. W. Peterson

The transitional mix of motive power at Connellsville is seen in this overall view. The line-up from left to right is 2–10–2 No. 6221, 0–8–0 No. 678, 2–8–2 No. 4174, and two unidentified 2–8–8–4's. Three Baldwin units are in the background.